MW01602143

NANDAY CONURE PARROT

Beginners Tips And Techniques To Care And Training Nanday Conure Parrot

JESSE WILSON

Table of Contents

Introductory

The Nanday Conure, also known as the Nanday Parakeet or Black-hooded Parakeet, is a species of South American parrot found in Bolivia, Brazil, and Argentina, among others. These parrots are recognized for their colorful and distinct appearance.

Here are some important traits and characteristics of Nanday Conure Parrots:

• Nanday Conures are medium-sized parrots with green plumage that predominates. They wear a black hood or mask that extends from their cranium to their chest and neck. Their wings and tail feathers are typically blue, and their quadriceps are tinged with red.

• They are typically between 12 and 13 inches (30-33 centimeters) long.

• Nanday Conures have a social and intelligent demeanor. They are known for their outgoing and lively nature. They appreciate interacting with their human companions and are capable of producing a variety of squawks, screeches, and other vocalizations.

• In the wild, they consume an assortment of grains, fruits, and vegetation. It is essential to provide captive parrots with a balanced diet consisting of premium parrot pellets, fresh fruits, and vegetables.

- With appropriate care and attention, Nanday Conures have a lifespan of several decades. They may live between 20 and 30 years, or even longer.

- Habitat: These parrots inhabit a variety of habitats in the outdoors, including forests, savannas, and even urban areas. They are adaptable and able to flourish in a variety of environments.

- In terms of their conservation status, Nanday Conures are

regarded as a species of least concern, which means they do not face significant challenges to their populations. However, like many parrot species, they are affected by habitat loss due to deforestation and the pet trade.

• Nanday Conures are occasionally maintained as pets due to their colorful plumage and engaging personalities. Those who are prepared for the responsibilities of caring for a parrot can find them to be amazing companions.

When considering a Nanday Conure as a pet, it is essential to be aware of their social and active nature, as they require frequent interaction, mental stimulation, and appropriate care to thrive. Additionally, prospective parrot owners should investigate and comprehend the long-term commitment and responsibilities associated with parrot ownership.

CHAPTER ONE
Physical Determinants

Nanday Conure Parrots (Nandayus nenday) have distinguishing morphological characteristics that allow them to be distinguished from other parrot species. Here are some important physical characteristics of Nanday Conures:

1. The dimension of Nanday Conures is medium-sized. From the tip of their beaks to the end of their tails, they are typically between 12 and 13 inches (30-33 centimeters) in length.

2. Their plumage is predominantly green, with several distinguishing color characteristics:

• Black Hood: One of their most distinctive characteristics is a black hood or mask that extends from their cranium to their neck and chest.

• Blue Wings and Tail: Nanday Conures have brilliantly blue feathers on their wings and tail. These blue feathers contrast dramatically with the bird's green torso and black hood.

• Red quadriceps: Another distinguishing characteristic is the red coloration on their quadriceps. This lends a splash of additional color to their appearance.

3. They use their strong, slightly curved beak for a variety of duties, including eating, climbing, and exploring.

4. Their irises are either dark brown or black.

5. Nanday Conures have robust legs and feet with zygodactyl toes, which means that two toes point forward and two toes point backward. This foot structure enables them to effectively grasp and manipulate objects.

6. Tail: Their tail feathers are long and have a squared-off or slightly convex shape.

7. Sexual Dimorphism: Nanday Conures lack significant sexual dimorphism, which makes it difficult to visually distinguish males and females based solely on their physical characteristics. Oftentimes, behavioral indicators and, in some instances, DNA testing are used to determine the sex of these birds.

8. Young Birds: Typically, juvenile Nanday Conures have less vivid colors than adults. Until they mature, their plumage may be duller and less distinct, and their black canopy may not be fully developed.

These features make Nanday Conures visually distinctive and appealing. Their vibrant appearance, especially the contrast between their green body, black hood, blue wings, and scarlet thighs, makes them popular among parrot enthusiasts and pet owners. When keeping them as pets, it is essential to remember that their attractive appearance is complemented by their engaging personalities and social nature.

Behavioral Features

Nanday Conure Parrots are well-known for their vivacious personalities and diverse array of behavioral traits, which can make them delightful, yet occasionally challenging, companions. Here are some of their most notable behavioral characteristics:

• Nanday Conures are exceptionally social birds. They thrive on interaction with humans and can develop strong attachments to their caretakers. They frequently take pleasure in being a member of the family and participating in various activities.

• These conures are well-known for their lively and energetic disposition. They are physically and mentally stimulating because they include puzzles and activities. Providing them with ample play and exercise opportunities is essential for their health.

• Nanday Conures are extremely vocal and can be boisterous at times. They generate a variety of sounds, such as squawks, screeches, chirps, and whistles. Potential owners should be aware that while their vocal nature can be endearing, it can also be boisterous and disruptive.

• Numerous Nanday Conures are affectionate birds that develop close relationships with their owners. They often appreciate physical contact, including cuddling and head scratching. It is essential to establish a relationship of trust with them through positive interactions.

• These parrots are intelligent and need mental stimulation to avoid becoming dull. Providing them with tools, puzzles, and the chance to learn new skills can keep their minds active.

• When it comes to their cage or preferred perches, Nanday Conures can be territorial. If they believe that their space is being invaded by humans or other animals, they may exhibit aggressive behavior.

• Like other parrots, Nanday Conures have a natural instinct to gnaw. It's essential to provide them with appropriate toys and objects to chew on to prevent them from damaging furniture or other household items.

• During molting (the process of shedding old feathers and growing new ones), the behavior of Nanday Conures may alter. Due to their distress, they may become more irritable or sensitive during this time.

• Training Capability: Nanday Conures are capable of learning techniques and commands. Positive reinforcement techniques are effective with these animals. Consistency, persistence, and rewards are essential for effective training.

• While Nanday Conures can be affectionate and playful, they are also capable of displaying aggressive behavior if they feel intimidated or provoked. This may consist of nipping or lunging. Understanding their body language and cues is essential to avoid confrontations.

• These birds flourish on routine and may experience anxiety if their daily schedule is disrupted. A consistent environment can enable them to feel safe.

• Some Nanday Conures have a propensity to scream loudly, particularly when they are seeking attention or feeling anxious. Training them to use more subdued vocalizations or redirecting their behavior can assist with this.

Potential Nanday Conure proprietors need to be aware of and

prepared for these behavioral characteristics. Providing a stimulating environment, social interaction, and training can help birds maintain a harmonious relationship with their human companions by channeling their energy. In addition, seeking advice from experienced bird proprietors or avian specialists can be beneficial for addressing specific behavioral issues.

CHAPTER TWO
Natural Environment And Range

The Nanday Conure (Nandayus nenday), also known as the Nanday Parakeet or Black-hooded Parakeet, is native to South America and can be found in a number of its countries. Its natural habitat and range include a variety of ecosystems. Here is a summary of their natural habitat and distribution:

1. Nanday Conures are indigenous to a number of South American countries, including:

• They are found in areas of eastern Bolivia in Bolivia.

• Brazil: They inhabit a variety of Brazilian regions, including the Amazon basin and portions of the southeast and northeastern coasts.

• Argentina: They are also found in the northern portion of Argentina, specifically in the Chaco region.

2. Nanday Conures are adaptable birds that inhabit a diversity of habitats throughout their range. These habitats consist of:

• Tropical and Subtropical Forests: They are prevalent in primary and secondary tropical and subtropical forests, including the Amazon rainforest.

• Savannas: Nanday Conures inhabit savannas, which feature open grasslands and dispersed trees.

• Urban and Agricultural Areas: It is known that these species can adapt to human-altered environments, such as urban and agricultural areas. They are permitted to inhabit cities, villages, and farmlands.

3. In their natural habitat, Nanday Conures are social birds that create flocks ranging in size from a few individuals to a large number of individuals.

They are extremely adaptable and can eat a variety of foods, including fruits, seeds, berries, and plants. It is also known that they visit agricultural fields to subsist on crops such as corn and sunflowers.

4. Breeding: Nanday Conures frequently nest in tree cavities, especially those tail large trees. They may also nest in termite colonies or other naturally occurring cavities. Breeding pairs labor together to raise their young, and after a few weeks, the chicks leave the nest.

It is essential to note that, although Nanday Conures are native to South

America, they have been introduced to other continents as pets or through accidental escapes. In some regions, feral populations have become established.

Nanday Conures are still relatively prevalent and are not considered endangered in their native range. However, as with many other parrot species, they are threatened by habitat loss due to deforestation and capture for the pet trade. To assure their continued existence in their natural habitat, conservation efforts and habitat preservation are crucial.

Getting Ready For Your Nanday Conure

As a companion animal, a Nanday Conure necessitates careful contemplation and planning. These animals have particular requirements and necessitate a long-term commitment.

Here are some measures to help you prepare for the arrival of a Nanday Conure:

• Start by conducting exhaustive research on Nanday Conures and their care requirements. Discover their diet, behavior, social needs, and prospective health problems.

Comprehend the responsibilities and difficulties associated with maintaining a parrot as a pet.

• Legal Considerations: Investigate your local and national parrot regulations. Some species of parrots are protected, and you may need permits or licenses to legally possess one.

• Choose a Reputable Breeder or Rescue: If you decide to acquire a Nanday Conure, select a reputable breeder or think about adopting from a parrot rescue group. Ensure the bird you select is healthy, well-adjusted, and from a reliable source.

• Purchase a spacious, well-constructed, and secure cage for your pet. Nanday Conures are active birds that require ample space for movement.

Provide various sized and material platforms to promote foot health. In addition, collect supplies such as containers for food and water, toys, and cage liners.

• Diet: Understand their dietary needs, which typically consist of high-quality parrot pellets, fresh fruits, vegetables, and occasional indulgences. Ensure a steady supply of potable water.

- You can parrot-proof your property by eliminating or securing potential hazards. This includes toxic plants, domestic chemicals, and items that the bird could potentially ingest or chew on. Nanday Conures are inquisitive and enjoy exploring their environment.

- Socialization and Interaction: Nanday Conures are extremely social, interaction-oriented birds. Plan to spend time with your bird daily, providing mental stimulation and physical exercise through playtime and training.

- Invest time in training and integrating your Nanday Conure into society. Positive reinforcement methods are effective with parrots. Training can aid in forming a bond, preventing behavioral issues, and teaching techniques and behaviors.

• Find a qualified avian veterinarian in your area and schedule routine examinations for your bird. Maintain an emergency fund for possible medical costs.

• Prepare for the commotion that Nanday Conures may generate. Their vocalizations may not be suitable for apartments or communal living spaces due to their volume. When appropriate, train them to use subdued vocalizations.

• Molting and Grooming: Understand the process of molting and be prepared for feather dust and possible behavioral changes during this time. If your bird cannot maintain its plumage on its own, you might need to assist with grooming.

• Long-Term Commitment: Keep in mind that the average tenure of a Nanday Conure is 20 years or more. Ensure you are prepared for the long-term commitment and responsibility of parrot ownership.

• Provide ample mental and physical stimulation via trinkets, puzzles, foraging opportunities, and time out of the cage. Mental stimulation is necessary to prevent apathy and behavioral issues in Nanday Conures.

• Consider joining local or online parrot owner organizations and communities. These resources can provide fellow parrot devotees with support, advice, and a sense of community.

Bringing a Nanday Conure into your household can be both a rewarding and challenging experience. Being well-prepared and dedicated to meeting your bird's requirements is essential for their health and happiness, as well as for fostering a close relationship between you and your feathered friend.

Bringing Home Your Nanday Conure

Bringing your Nanday Conure home is an exhilarating but essential step on the path to becoming a pet owner. Follow these steps to ensure a smooth transition and a positive start to your bird's new existence in your home:

1. Prepare the Habitat and Cage:

• Place the cage in a quiet, secure, and comfortable area of your residence. Avoid exposing it to direct sunlight and drafts.

• Ensure that the cage is outfitted with varying-sized and -material perches, food and water dishes, and trinkets for mental stimulation.

2. Quarantine: If you have other birds, you must quarantine your new Nanday Conure for at least 30 days in a separate room or area to prevent the transmission of disease. This allows you to observe the health and behavior of your new bird before introducing it to other species.

3. Adaptation Phase:

• Permit your Nanday Conure to acclimate to its new environment without excessive interaction at first. This helps reduce the bird's tension.

• Speak softly and calmly to your bird to enable it to become accustomed to your voice.

4. Diet Modification:

• To reduce stress, continue feeding your bird the same diet it had with the breeder or previous proprietor.

• Transition gradually to the diet you intend to provide over the course of several weeks.

5. Veterinary Examination:

• Schedule an appointment with an avian veterinarian as soon as possible after bringing your Nanday Conure home. This enables you to establish a health baseline and address any prospective health issues.

6. Socialization and Attachment:

• Spend time in close proximity to the cage, conversing with the bird and offering treats through the bars in order to build trust and familiarity.

• Gradually open the cage door and permit your bird to leave on its own accord. Avoid initially forcing the animal to exit its cage.

7. Education and Interaction:

• Commence training with positive reinforcement to teach fundamental commands and tricks.

• Increase the amount of time your avian spends out of its cage and interacting with you as it becomes more comfortable.

8. Environmental protection and safety:

• Parrot-proof your residence by removing potential hazards such as poisonous plants, chemicals, and items that your bird may chew on or ingest.

• Ensure that all windows and doors are locked to prevent accidental egress.

9. Consistent Habit:

• Establish a daily routine that includes feeding, recreation, and interaction. Parrots flourish on consistency.

10.Sound Abatement:

• Anticipate the decibel level of a Nanday Conure and help your bird learn when to use quieter vocalizations.

11. Augmentation and Stimulation:

• Provide a variety of games and puzzles to stimulate your bird's mind and body.

• Provide opportunities for foraging to encourage natural behaviors.

12. Be patient and observe:

• Have patience as your Nanday Conure acclimate to its new environment. It can take time for birds to feel at ease.

• Keep a close eye on your bird's health and behavior, as any sudden changes may indicate a problem that requires attention.

13. Join a Parrot Community: Consider connecting with local or online parrot owner communities or organizations in order to receive support and advice from avian experts.

When you bring a Nanday Conure into your household, you embark on a long and rewarding journey. Developing a close relationship with your bird requires time, perseverance, and consistency.

You can ensure that your Nanday Conure thrives as a cherished member of your family by providing a safe and affectionate environment and meeting its physical and emotional requirements.

CHAPTER THREE
Caring For A Contented And Healthy Nanday Conure

Maintaining a happy and healthy Nanday Conure necessitates continuous care for its physical, mental, and emotional health. It is essential to provide these social and intelligent birds with a stimulating and nurturing environment. Here are some suggestions for maintaining the health of your Nanday Conure:

1. Diet and nourishment:

• Provide a balanced diet of premium parrot pellets and fresh fruits and vegetables. Offer a variety of foods to ensure that your bird receives all of the necessary nutrients.

• Limit your consumption of sugary and fatty delights, as they can cause health problems such as obesity.

2. Availability of liquids:

• Always provide fresh, clean water in a dish that is stable and readily accessible.

• Observe your bird's water consumption to ensure it stays adequately hydrated.

3. The Cage and Its Setting:

• Keep the cage tidy by removing droppings and uneaten food on a regular basis.

• Rotate objects and keep them clean to prevent boredom.

• Provide a secure and comfortable environment with suitable perches, hiding places, and sleeping accommodations.

4. Interpersonal Interaction:

• Devote daily quality time to your Nanday Conure. They depend on social interaction and may develop depression in its absence.

• Participate in interactive play and training sessions to strengthen your relationship with your bird.

5. Cognitive Stimulation:

• Provide your bird with an assortment of tools, puzzles, and foraging opportunities to keep it mentally active.

• Rotate objects frequently in order to sustain interest.

6. Playtime and Exercise:

• Let your Nanday Conure out of its cage for daily exercise and enjoyment in a bird-safe environment.

• Provide a climbing structure or branches secure for birds for climbing and exercise.

7. Education and Enrichment:

• Continue training with positive reinforcement to teach your bird techniques and commands that stimulate its problem-solving abilities.

• Teach your bird to hunt for sustenance in order to engage its natural instincts.

8. Sound Abatement:

• Be prepared for your Nanday Conure's vocalizations, and work with them to teach them appropriate vocalization times.

• Use positive reinforcement to encourage calm conduct.

9. Consistent Veterinary Care:

• Schedule annual examinations with an avian veterinarian to monitor your bird's health and detect potential problems early.

• Maintain a record of your bird's weight and general health.

10. The art of grooming:

• Trim the claws and wings of your bird as necessary to prevent injury.

• Offer opportunities for bathing, such as a shallow dish of water or a spray fountain.

11. Respect Their Space:

• Recognize and respect your bird's need for personal space. Avoid imposing interaction on a bird that prefers solitude.

12. Sustainable Environment:

• Ensure your home environment is devoid of potential dangers for a curious avian, such as toxic plants and chemicals.

13. Patience and Comprehension:

• Be patient with your Nanday Conure, particularly during anxious or stressful situations.

• Comprehend their body language and vocalizations in order to better address their requirements and concerns.

14. Relationships with Other Birds:

• If you have multiple birds, you must ensure their compatibility and observe their interactions to avoid conflicts.

15. Long-Term Dedication:

- Keep in mind that Nanday Conures are long-lived, so be prepared for a lifelong commitment to their care and well-being.

By providing a compassionate and stimulating environment, consistent care, and routine health examinations, you can raise a Nanday Conure that is a thriving member of your family.

Physiology And Diet

For the health and well-being of your Nanday Conure, it is essential to provide it with the proper diet. A balanced diet provides the nutrients necessary for growth, vitality, and general health trace elements. Here are some feeding instructions for your Nanday Conure:

1. Pellets --

• Your Nanday Conure's diet should be based on commercial parrot pellets of the highest quality. These granules contain essential vitamins, minerals, and nutrients.

- Select pellets formulated for medium to large parrots, and opt for brands that use natural ingredients without added colors or flavors.

- Pellets should make up approximately 70-80% of your bird's daily diet.

2. Fresh Vegetables and Fruits:

- Offer fresh fruits and vegetables as a supplement to the pellet diet. These foods are an excellent source of vitamins and minerals.

- Fruits that are suitable include apples, pears, berries, oranges, and papayas.

• Carrots, broccoli, spinach, kale, and bell peppers are superb vegetable choices.

• Ensure the fruits and vegetables are washed thoroughly and cut into small, manageable portions. Remove all fruit seeds and shells.

3. Protein Sources:

• Nanday Conures require protein for muscle growth and good health. Offer cooked eggs, lean cooked meat (chicken, turkey), and prepared legumes (lentils or beans).

• Limit animal protein consumption to 10 to 15 percent of their diet.

4. Nutritious Snacks:

• Whole grains (cooked quinoa, brown rice) and small quantities of nuts (almonds, walnuts, or pistachios) can be offered as treats on occasion. Due to their high fat content, almonds should be consumed with caution and in moderation.

5. Avoid Poisonous Foods:

• Certain substances are toxic to birds and should be avoided at all costs. These include chocolate, caffeine, alcohol, avocado, and high-sodium, high-sugar, or high-fat foods.

• Use caution when consuming foods with cavities or seeds, as they may contain cyanide and should be removed.

6. Presentation of Food:

• Present food in a variety of methods to pique the interest of your Nanday Conure. To make mealtimes more engaging, you can offer fresh foods of various sizes, shapes, and colors.

7. Pure Water:

• Ensure that your bird has access to clean, fresh water at all times. Every day, the water should be replaced to maintain hygiene.

8. Nutritional Supplements:

• In the majority of cases, a well-balanced diet consisting of pellets and raw foods should provide all the required nutrients. However, you can provide vitamin and mineral supplements if your avian physician suggests cements and vitamins.

9. Observe Food Intake:

• Monitor your Nanday Conure's food consumption. To avoid overfeeding or underfeeding, adjust portion proportions based on activity level and weight.

10. Dietary Schedule:

• Establish a regular meal schedule to provide consistency and structure for your bird.

Keeping in mind that Nanday Conures have distinct dietary preferences, it may take some time to identify their preferred foods. In addition, their dietary requirements may change over the course of their lives; therefore, consult with an avian veterinarian for specific guidance and routine checkups to ensure that their nutritional requirements are met.

CHAPTER FOUR
Reproduction And Reproduction

Breeding and reproduction of Nanday Conures (Nandayus nenday) can be rewarding, but it requires meticulous planning and an understanding of their natural behaviors. If you're interested in breeding Nanday Conures, you should consider the following:

1. Maturity and Relationship:

• Nanday Conures typically attain sexual maturity between the ages of 2 and 3 years.

• When choosing breeding partners, it is essential to select birds that are healthy and unrelated. Avoid inbreeding because it can cause genetic issues.

2. The housing:

• Provide an environment suitable for breeding, which typically consists of a larger breeding cage or a distinct aviary. The enclosure must provide nesting boxes or other nesting locations.

• Nesting boxes should be of an appropriate dimension, secure, and composed of non-hazardous materials (such as wood). They should have an access opening and a detachable lid for inspection and maintenance.

3. Diet and Wellness:

• Ensure that the reproductive pair is in excellent health and consuming a balanced diet with a focus on calcium-rich foods to promote egg production.

• Closely observe the birds for any indications of illness or stress.

4. Nesting Supplies:

• Provide the female with nest-building materials, such as wood sawdust, straw, and other soft materials.

5. Intimacy and Bonding:

• Nanday Conure pairs often engage in courtship behaviors, such as mutual preening and feeding each other. These behaviors indicate their preparedness to mate and strengthen their bond.

6. Laying Eggs and Incubation:

• After laying an average of 3-5 eggs per brood, the female will begin incubating them. The incubation period typically lasts 23-28 days. that.

• During this period, the female will spend the majority of her time in the nesting box, maintaining the eggs' temperature.

7. Parental Duties:

• Both the male and female perform significant roles in egg and chick care. They take shifts incubating the eggs and feeding the newborn chicks.

• It is essential to provide the breeding pair with a balanced diet so they can sufficiently nourish their young.

8. Feeding by Hand and Weaning:

• If you intend to nurture the chicks by hand, you may need to remove them from the nest after a few weeks. For guidance on hand-feeding and weaning, consult an experienced avian breeder or veterinarian.

9. Condition Monitoring:

• Regularly examine the nest for any issues, such as dead eggs, chicks with health problems, or aggression between the parents.

• Maintain a tidy nesting area to prevent the accumulation of waste and disease.

10. Ethical and Legal Considerations:

• Familiarize yourself with local and national laws governing the propagation and sale of parrots. Ensure that your reproduction practices are legal and moral.

Breeding Nanday Conures requires dedication, effort, and avian care expertise. If you are considering breeding these birds, it is recommended that you obtain advice from experienced breeders or avian veterinarians, who can offer specific advice and assistance throughout the process.

Breeding should only be pursued if you are prepared for the responsibilities it entails and have a plan to place any progeny in suitable homes.

Frequent Health Concerns

Like all parrots, Nanday Conure parrots are susceptible to a variety of health problems. Providing adequate care, a clean environment, and routine veterinary examinations can aid in preventing a number of these issues. Here are several common health concerns that proprietors of Nanday Conures should be aware of.

• Feather Plucking: Feather plucking may be a symptom of underlying health issues, such as skin irritation, allergies, parasites, or tension. It is essential to identify and address the underlying cause.

• Nanday Conures are susceptible to respiratory infections, which are frequently brought on by exposure to drafts, low temperatures, or dusty environments. There may be sneezing, wheezing, nasal discharge, and labored breathing as symptoms.

• Gastrointestinal Problems: An improper diet, bacterial or fungal infections, or the ingestion of toxic substances can cause digestive issues. Symptoms may include diarrhea, vomiting, and altered feces.

• Psittacine Beak and Feather Disease (PBFD) is a viral disease that can impair the immune system, feathers, and beak of parrots. Symptoms include anomalous feather growth, deformed beaks, and a weakened immune system. No treatment exists for PBFD.

• Aspergillosis is a fungal infection that can affect the lungs and other organs. Birds may exhibit symptoms such as difficulty breathing, coughing, or behavioral alterations.

• External parasites such as mites and ticks can cause irritation to the skin and plumage. Worms and other internal organisms can affect the digestive system. Regular veterinary examinations can detect and treat these conditions.

• Obesity: Overfeeding and a diet high in fatty or saccharine foods can cause obesity in Nanday Conures, which can lead to a variety of health issues. Encourage a balanced diet and physical activity.

• Hypovitaminosis A: A vitamin A deficiency can result in eye and respiratory issues. Provide a fruit and vegetable-rich diet to prevent this deficiency.

• Lead Poisoning: Like other parrot species, Nanday Conures can accidentally ingest lead or other toxic substances found in household items or poorly painted toys. Be mindful of your bird's environment and avoid these dangers.

Birds are prone to injuries including fractured wings and beaks. Take precautions to prevent catastrophes in the environment of your bird.

• Stress-Related Problems: Stress can impair birds' immune systems, making them more susceptible to a variety of health issues. Ensure the safety and comfort of your Nanday Conure's environment.

• Aspects Related to Aging: As Nanday Conures age, they may be susceptible to age-related ailments such as arthritis or a weakened immune system. Regular veterinary care becomes even more crucial as animals age.

Remember that early detection and prompt treatment are essential for addressing health problems in Nanday Conures.

Regular checkups with an avian veterinarian, a well-balanced diet, a clean living environment, and the provision of mental and physical stimulation are essential for their health and well-being. If you observe any symptoms of illness or unusual behavior in your Nanday Conure, you should seek veterinary care immediately.

CHAPTER FIVE
Adoption And Ownership Responsibly

Responsible ownership and adoption of a Nanday Conure, or any other companion, requires a lifelong commitment to providing a loving and nurturing environment. Here are some essential principles of responsible adoption and ownership:

• Education and Research: Before acquiring a Nanday Conure, conduct extensive research on the species, including its care requirements, behavior, and potential difficulties.

Prepare yourself for the long-term commitment of parrot care.

• Ethical and Legal Considerations: Ensure compliance with local and national laws and regulations pertaining to pet ownership and the harboring of exotic birds. Avoid contributing to the illegal wildlife trade.

• Consider adopting a Nanday Conure from a reputable rescue organization or a bird in need from a local shelter. Adoption is a compassionate choice that provides birds in need with a caring home.

• Select a Healthy Bird: o When adopting or purchasing a Nanday Conure, select a bird that appears active and vigilant. It is essential to begin with a solid base.

• Veterinary Care: Develop a rapport with an avian veterinarian and schedule regular checkups for your Nanday Conure. Routine veterinary care is necessary for early disease detection and prevention.

• Nutrition and Diet: Provide a balanced diet that meets the nutritional requirements of your bird. Offer fresh fruits, vegetables, and pellets of superior quality.

Avoid offering poisonous delicacies to birds.

• Safe Environment: Ensure your residence is safe for your Nanday Conure by parrot-proofing it. Remove potential hazards such as poisonous plants, chemicals, and items that your bird could ingest or gnaw on.

• Nanday Conures are extremely social birds that require daily interaction and mental stimulation. Spend time with your bird playing, training, and connecting.

• Mental and Physical Stimulation: Provide diversions, puzzles, and opportunities for mental and physical exercise to prevent boredom and promote the health and happiness of the bird.

• Teach your Nanday Conure appropriate behavior and tricks using positive reinforcement training techniques. Training strengthens your relationship with your creature.

• Noise Management: o Anticipate the noise level of Nanday Conures and take the necessary measures to manage it, particularly in shared living spaces.

- Interpret your bird's requirements and emotions by interpreting their body language and vocalizations. Respect their unique preferences and dispositions.

Be prepared for the long-term commitment of caring for a Nanday Conure, which can live for at least 20 years. Ensure that you can meet their needs for the rest of their lives.

Join parrot owner communities or clubs to communicate with others who share your passion. These communities can offer assistance, guidance, and a sense of belonging.

Preparedness for Emergencies: o Have an emergency plan in place, including access to an avian veterinarian and knowledge of what to do in the event of accidents or maladies.

For the well-being of Nanday Conures and all companions, responsible ownership and adoption are essential. You can ensure that your Nanday Conure thrives and lives a fulfilling life as a cherished member of your family by providing affection, appropriate care, and a safe, stimulating environment.

Conclusion

Owning and providing for a Nanday Conure is a rewarding and fulfilling experience, but there are responsibilities involved. These vibrant parrots require affection, care, and a nurturing environment in order to thrive.

As a responsible pet owner, you must provide adequate nutrition, routine veterinary care, mental and physical stimulation, and a secure living environment.

It also requires a comprehension of their distinct behaviors and requirements, as well as a willingness to make a long-term commitment, as Nanday Conures can live for over two decades.

Whether you adopt a Nanday Conure or purchase one from a reputable source, keep in mind that each bird has its own unique personality and preferences.

Building a strong bond with your Nanday Conure through positive interaction, training, and consideration for their well-being is essential for ensuring that they live a happy and healthy existence.

By educating yourself, seeking advice when necessary, and

accepting the responsibilities of ownership, you can provide a loving and enriching existence for your Nanday Conure, nurturing a long-lasting, mutually beneficial relationship.

THE END

Made in United States
North Haven, CT
11 April 2025

67860705R00048